PLACES IN MY COMMUNITY

AIRPORT

John Willis

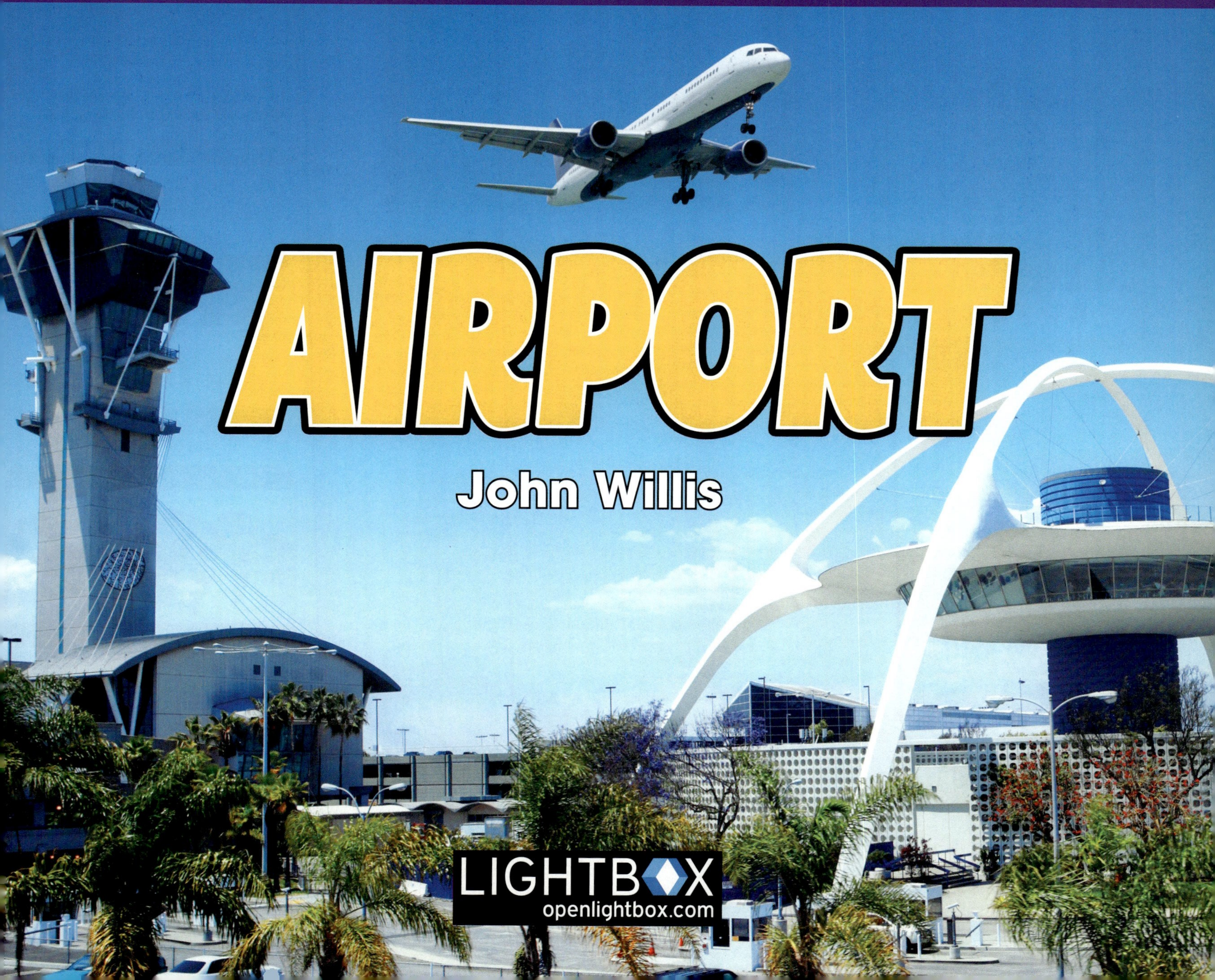

LIGHTBOX
openlightbox.com

LIGHTBOX

Go to **www.openlightbox.com** and enter this book's unique code.

ACCESS CODE

LBR34455

Lightbox is an all-inclusive digital solution for the teaching and learning of curriculum topics in an original, groundbreaking way. Lightbox is based on National Curriculum Standards.

OPTIMIZED FOR

- ✓ TABLETS
- ✓ WHITEBOARDS
- ✓ COMPUTERS
- ✓ AND MUCH MORE!

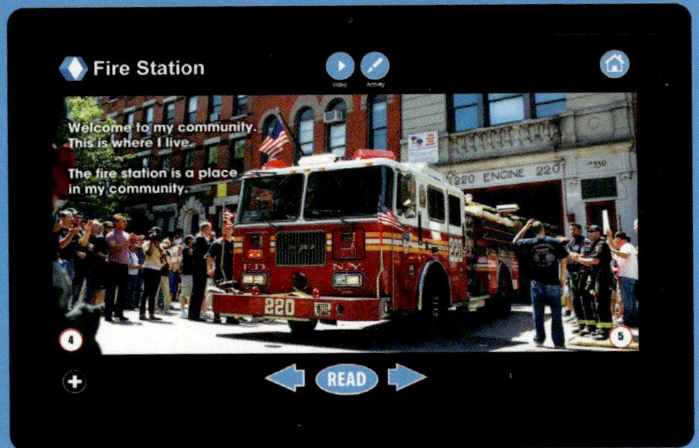

STANDARD FEATURES OF LIGHTBOX

 **AUDIO** High-quality narration using text-to-speech system

 **VIDEOS** Embedded high-definition video clips

 **ACTIVITIES** Printable PDFs that can be emailed and graded

 **WEBLINKS** Curated links to external, child-safe resources

 **SLIDESHOWS** Pictorial overviews of key concepts

 **INTERACTIVE MAPS** Interactive maps and aerial satellite imagery

 **QUIZZES** Ten multiple choice questions that are automatically graded and emailed for teacher assessment

KEY WORDS Matching key concepts to their definitions

VIDEOS

WEBLINKS

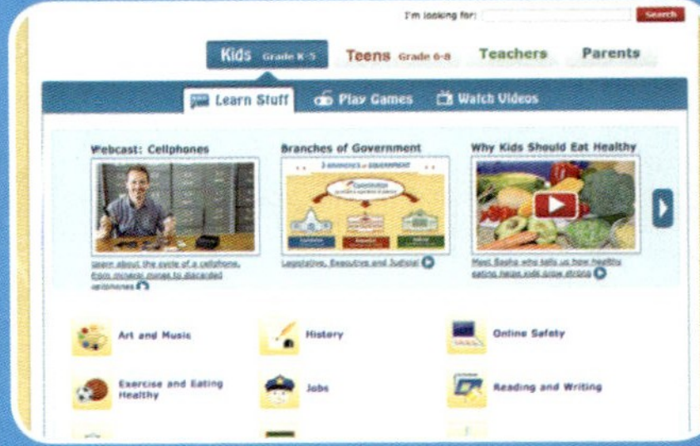

SLIDESHOWS

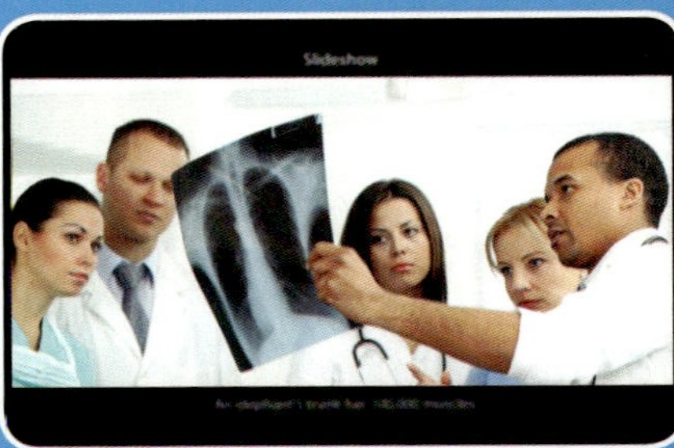

QUIZZES

AIRPORT

In this book, you will learn about

airports

the people who work there

why they are important

and much more!

Welcome to my community.
This is where I live.

The airport is a place in my community.

American
910
American
24312
American
321
CR7 73-8
ERJ

The airport is a place where airplanes come and go.

People get on and off airplanes from a building called a terminal.

More than **2 million** people in the United States get on planes every day.

An airline clerk helps passengers check in and get their tickets.

She weighs a passenger's luggage. Then, she sends it to be stored on the plane.

Airport security checks people's bags and pockets by using special machines.

This helps keep passengers safe.

The **largest airport** in the United States is in **Atlanta, Georgia**.

Baggage handlers move luggage on and off an airplane.

They make sure that the right luggage is placed on each airplane.

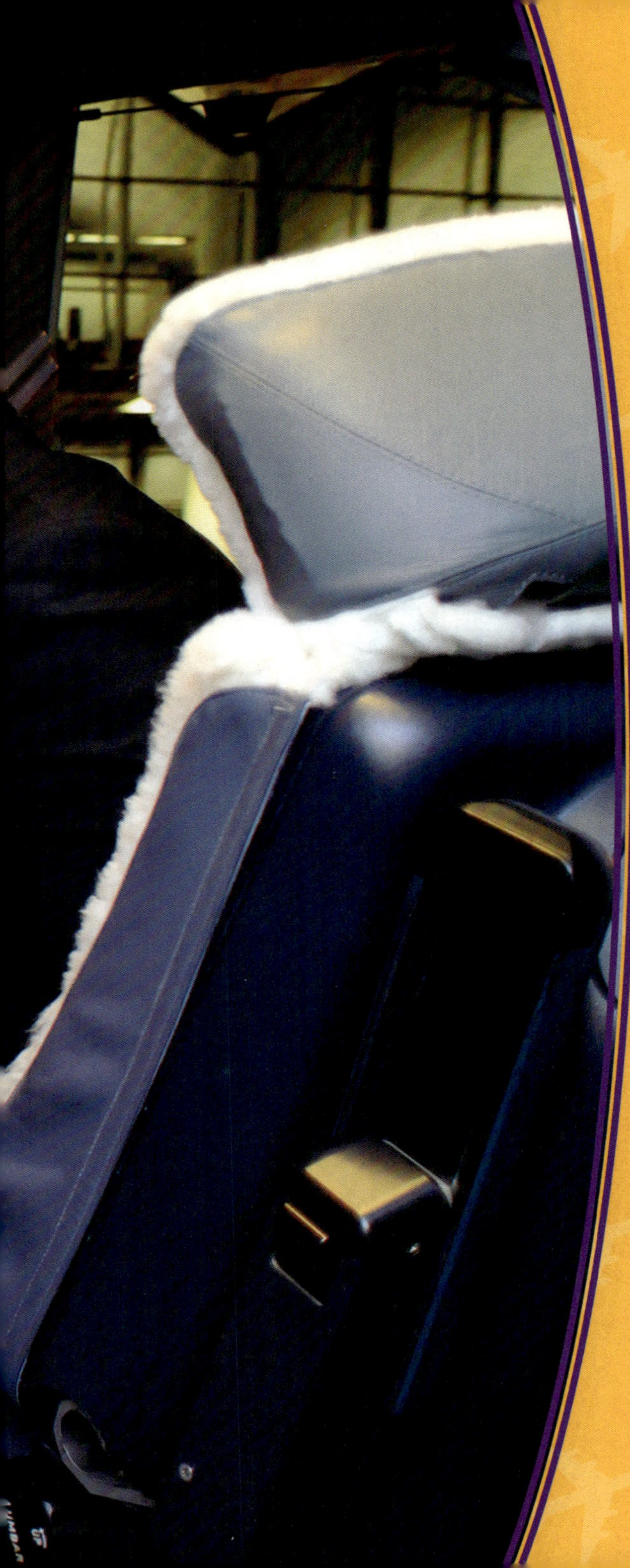

Pilots fly the airplanes. More than one pilot works on each airplane.

The pilot in charge is called the captain.

The **first** airline service flew between St. Petersburg, Florida, and Tampa, Florida, in **1914**.

Air traffic controllers work in tall towers. They use computers to help pilots fly and land their airplanes safely.

The **tallest** air traffic control tower in the United States is **398 feet** tall.

RYANAIR

My class will take a field trip to the airport. We will learn about many different kinds of airplanes.

We might even get to sit inside the cockpit of an airplane.

People from all over the world use airports to visit their friends and family.

Airports help bring people from different communities together.

See what you have learned about airports and the people that work at them.

Which of these pictures does not show an airport?

KEY WORDS

Research has shown that as much as 65 percent of all written material published in English is made up of 300 words. These 300 words cannot be taught using pictures or learned by sounding them out. They must be recognized by sight. This book contains 60 common sight words to help young readers improve their reading fluency and comprehension. This book also teaches young readers several important content words, such as proper nouns. These words are paired with pictures to aid in learning and improve understanding.

Page	Sight Words First Appearance
4	I, is, live, my, this, to, where
5	a, in, place, the
7	and, come, day, every, from, get, go, more, off, on, people, than
8	an, helps, their
9	be, it, she, then
10	by, keep
12	move
13	each, make, right, that, they
15	between, first, one, works
16	land, use
18	about, different, kinds, learn, many, of, take, we, will
19	even, might
20	all, family, over, world
21	together

Page	Content Words First Appearance
4	community
5	airport
7	airplanes, building, terminal
8	airline clerk, passengers, tickets
9	luggage
10	bags, machines, pockets, security
12	baggage handlers
15	captain, pilots
16	air traffic controllers, computers, towers
18	class, field trip
19	cockpit
20	friends

Published by Smartbook Media Inc.
350 5th Avenue, 59th Floor New York, NY 10118
Website: www.openlightbox.com

Library of Congress Cataloging-in-Publication Data

Names: Willis, John, 1989- author.
Title: Airport / John Willis.
Description: New York, NY : Smartbook Media Inc., [2016] | Series: Places in my community | Includes index.
Identifiers: LCCN 2016051531 (print) | LCCN 2016051886 (ebook) | ISBN 9781510518773 (hard cover : alk. paper) | ISBN 9781510518780 (multi-user ebk.)
Subjects: LCSH: Airports--Juvenile literature. | Airports--Employees--Juvenile literature.
Classification: LCC TL725.15 .W55 2016 (print) | LCC TL725.15 (ebook) | DDC 387.7/36--dc23
LC record available at https://lccn.loc.gov/2016051531

Printed in the United States of America in Brainerd, Minnesota
1 2 3 4 5 6 7 8 9 0 20 19 18 17 16

122016
111816

Project Coordinator: Jared Siemens
Designer: Ana María Vidal

The publisher acknowledges iStock, Alamy, Getty Images, Shutterstock, and Dreamstime as its primary image suppliers for this title.